c.1

DATE DUE		$ 14.95
OCT 0 2 1997	FE 19 02	
OCT 17 199	AP 23 04	
OCT 27 199	SE 24 '04	
FEB 17 1998	OC 08 '04	
OCT 2 0 199	NO 17 '06	
FEB 05 199	11-6-07	
FEB 19 1999	11-23-07	
APR 16 1999		
NOV 05 1999		
FE 12 02		
MR 10 04		
JAN 25 2002		

92
MAR

Wilner, Barry
Dan Marino : 13

FOOTBALL LEGENDS

Troy Aikman

Terry Bradshaw

Jim Brown

Dan Marino

Joe Montana

Joe Namath

Walter Payton

Jerry Rice

Barry Sanders

Deion Sanders

Emmitt Smith

Steve Young

CHELSEA HOUSE PUBLISHERS

DAN MARINO

Barry Wilner

Introduction by
Chuck Noll

CHELSEA HOUSE PUBLISHERS
New York · Philadelphia

Produced by Daniel Bial and Associates
New York, New York

Picture research by Alan Gottlieb
Cover illustration by Bill Vann

3 5 7 9 8 6 4 2

Wilner, Barry.
    Dan Marino / by Barry Wilner
    p. cm. — (Football legends)
    Includes bibliographical references and index.
    ISBN 0-7910-2458-X
    1. Marino, Dan, 1961-   —Juvenile literature. 2. Football
players—United States—Biography—Juvenile literature.
3. Miami Dolphins (Football team)—Juvenile literature.
4. Marino, Dan, 1961-   . [1. Football players.] I. Title.
II. Series.
GV939.M29W46 1996
796.332'092—dc20
    [B]   95-30123
                                                      CIP
                                                      AC

CONTENTS

A WINNING ATTITUDE

Chuck Noll

Don't ever fall into the trap of believing, "I could never do that. And I won't even try—I don't want to embarrass myself." After all, most top athletes had no idea what they could accomplish when they were young. A secret to the success of every star quarterback and sure-handed receiver is that they tried. If they had not tried, if they had not persevered, they would never have discovered how far they could go and how much they could achieve.

You can learn about trying hard and overcoming challenges by being a sports fan. Or you can take part in organized sports at any level, in any capacity. The student messenger at my high school is now president of a university. A reserve ballplayer who got very little playing time in high school now owns a very successful business. Both of them benefited from the lesson of perseverance that sports offers. The main point is that you don't have to be a Hall of Fame athlete to reap the benefits of participating in sports.

In math class, I learned that the whole is equal to the sum of its parts. But that is not always the case when you are dealing with people. Sports has taught me that the whole is either greater than or less than the sum of its parts, depending on how well the parts work together. And how the parts work together depends on how they really understand the concept of teamwork.

Most people believe that teamwork is a fifty-fifty proposition. But true teamwork is seldom, if ever, fifty-fifty. Teamwork is *whatever it takes to get the job done.* There is no time for the measurement of contributions, no time for anything but concentrating on your job.

One year, my Pittsburgh Steelers were playing the Houston Oilers in the Astrodome late in the season, with the division championship on the line. Our offensive line was hard hit by the flu, our starting quarterback was out with an injury, and we were having difficulty making a first down. There was tremendous pressure on our defense to perform well—and they rose to the occasion. If the players on the defensive unit had been measuring their contribution against the offense's contribution, they would have given up and gone home. Instead, with a "whatever it takes" attitude, they increased their level of concentration and performance, forced turnovers, and got the ball into field goal range for our offense. Thanks to our defense's winning attitude, we came away with a victory.

Believing in doing whatever it takes to get the job done is what separates a successful person from someone who is not as successful. Nobody can give you this winning outlook; you have to develop it. And I know from experience that it can be learned and developed on the playing field.

My favorite people on the football field have always been offensive linemen and defensive backs. I say this because it takes special people to perform well in jobs in which there is little public recognition when they are doing things right but are thrust into the spotlight as soon as they make a mistake. That is exactly what happens to a lineman whose man sacks the quarterback or a defensive back who lets his receiver catch a touchdown pass. They know the importance of being part of a group that believes in teamwork and does not point fingers at one another.

Sports can be a learning situation as much as it can be fun. And that's why I say, "Get involved. Participate."

CHUCK NOLL, the Pittsburgh Steelers head coach from 1969–91, led his team to four Super Bowl victories—the most by any coach. Widely respected as an innovator on both offense and defense, Noll was inducted into the Pro Football Hall of Fame in 1993.

1

DAN'S GREATEST GAME

O n September 4, 1994, Dan Marino led the Miami Dolphins onto the field and felt a strange emotion. For one of the few times in his life, he felt unsure. Usually he knew how good he was and how much he could do as a quarterback. He had shown he could do things passing a football that no one else could do.

Yet on this warm afternoon, Marino was wondering if he still had it. He hadn't played in a meaningful game in nearly a year. On October 10, 1993, he had suffered the first major injury of his life, a torn Achilles tendon in his heel. Marino underwent surgery and needed many months of rehabilitation to get back the strength and mobility in his leg.

Marino started out well in exhibition games but got worse as the preseason wore on. He had a poor outing in the final warm-up, a game

Before the start of the 1994 season, Dan Marino was worried whether he had fully recovered from the injury he had suffered the previous year.

against the Minnesota Vikings. Some people were saying that backup quarterback Bernie Kosar should start the season.

Coach Don Shula knew better. He had won more games in NFL history than any other coach, and he understood that you don't bench as great a player as Dan Marino after a few exhibition games. "Dan is our quarterback," Shula said. "We won't judge him by what has happened in the preseason. I have faith in Dan."

In 1994, Marino celebrated his 12th year as a pro. He owned numerous passing records and was closing in on many others. But Marino had never had a major injury before. He was 34 years old; most quarterbacks have been forced to retire by that age. Did he still have what it takes to succeed in the National Football League (NFL)?

Marino rewarded his coach's faith in short order. The first game of the regular season pitted the Dolphins against a conference rival, the New England Patriots. The Patriots quickly scored the game's first touchdown. Marino erased that lead with a 64-yard touchdown pass to Mark Ingram. The Dolphins had signed the former New York Giants wide receiver as a free agent in 1993. He arrived in Miami saying, "I love the idea of playing catch with Dan Marino."

The Patriots outscored the Dolphins, 14–3, to take a 21–10 lead as their second-year quarterback, Drew Bledsoe, matched Marino's numbers. Bill Parcells, New England's coach, fashioned a pass-oriented offense for his team, often calling on his quarterback to throw 40 or even 50 passes a game.

"He's going to be a great quarterback," Marino said of Bledsoe. "He has an excellent arm."

Did Bledsoe remind Dan of somebody? Maybe Marino himself?

"I don't know about that," Marino said with a smile. "We'll see."

The crowd in packed Joe Robbie Stadium stood and cheered as Marino found tight end Keith Jackson for a 26-yard score. Terry Kirby ran for a 2-point conversion to make it 21–18, but Bledsoe soon followed with his third touchdown pass of the day.

In his greatest game, Dan Marino threw for 473 yards and five touchdowns, leading his Dolphins into a tremendous come-from-behind victory over the New England Patriots.

Marino answered with his third touchdown pass, a 54-yarder to Irving Fryar, a wide receiver who had played many years for the Patriots.

When the Dolphins had the ball at the start of the fourth quarter, they pulled out an old trick play: the flea flicker. After taking the snap from center, Marino handed off to Kirby, who headed into the line. Suddenly Kirby stopped and flipped the ball back to Marino. The defensive backs had pulled up for the run, leaving Fryar wide open. Marino's pass covered 50 yards and Fryar danced into the end zone.

"It worked perfectly," Marino said. "That was a fun play."

The Dolphins led for the first time, 32–28. But there were 14 minutes to go, and Miami's defense was having a rough time on the muddy field. The Patriots took the kickoff and returned the ball to their 33 yardline. Less than three minutes later, Bledsoe threw a 23-yard pass to Ray Crittenden for the go-ahead score. Now both quarterbacks had thrown four touchdown passes on the day.

Miami's defensive players left the field with their heads hanging. But they also had hope because they had Marino on their side. "When you come out of a game like this," linebacker Bryan Cox said, "you don't say the offense played well and we didn't, so we should feel bad."

Cox knew that Marino could make all of the defenders feel good. Dan knew it, too. "There was a lot of time left, and we have moved the ball all game," Marino said. "We all believed we'd get it done."

Down 35–32, Miami took the ball at its 20. Marino began chipping away. Nearly every Dolphins back, wideout, and tight end got to contribute. In all, seven different receivers caught passes in the game.

The Miami machine reached the New England 35, where it faced a fourth down needing five yards for a first down. The Dolphins could have gone for a tying field goal, but Shula wanted the game in Marino's hands.

"It would have been a 52-yard field goal in the messiest part of the field," Shula said. "I wanted to take our shot with Dan. He's done it so many times for us. I felt he would do it again."

So did just about anyone who has seen some of Marino's many miracles.

Fryar lined up on the right. Marino looked over the line and saw a defense that placed cornerback Rod Smith in one-on-one coverage. Both Dan and Irving knew what to do.

"It was a do-or-die situation and I had man coverage," Fryar said. "Dan has played in the league long enough to realize who had the man coverage, and he went to me."

Instead of going to Fryar short, though, Marino and his receiver went deep. Fryar jetted past his man, Marino got him the ball, and Fryar went into the end zone standing up.

"After he read the defense, he still had to make the pass," Fryar said. "He threw it perfect, and that is a tough throw on fourth down near the end of the game."

Bledsoe and company couldn't come back from that blow. The final score was Miami 39, New England 35.

In the fourth quarter, Marino completed 8 of 13 passes for 179 yards and 2 touchdowns. In the game, he had set a few league records and some team marks. Dan had answered all the questions about his health, his comeback, and his skills.

"I felt pretty good about what I did," he said. "It's hard to imagine doing this right off the bat."

Marino's five touchdown passes gave him 18 games with at least four touchdown throws: an NFL record. It was his first five-touchdown game in six years, but the sixth in his pro career.

In the course of the game, Marino threw his 300th career touchdown pass. Fran Tarkenton is the only other quarterback ever to throw that many.

Marino set another record: his 473 yards were the most for a Dolphins quarterback on an opening day.

"When you think about it," said Fryar, who caught five passes for 211 yards, "that was one of the great performances ever by an athlete."

It was the most memorable of Dan's life.

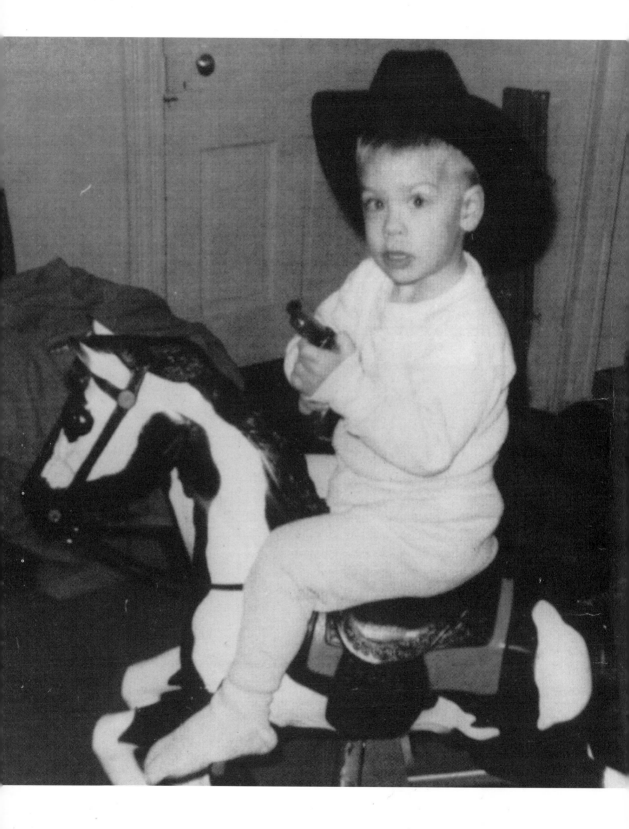

2

YOUNG DAN

When Dan Marino was growing up in the Oakland section of Pittsburgh, Pennsylvania, he dreamed of doing great things as a pro athlete. But his dreams centered on him winning the World Series, not the Super Bowl.

Back in his younger days, especially his teenage years, Marino's first choice was the diamond, not the gridiron. "As much as I liked football when I was young," he recalls, "I liked baseball even better. Everyone thinks I was a pitcher, I guess because they see how strong my arm is, and I could throw the ball well. I had a pretty lively fastball. But I could hit, too, and I really liked hitting."

Dan played so much baseball that when it came time to take his driving test, he did so in his baseball uniform. "We were between games of a doubleheader," he explains.

Marino was so good at baseball that he was drafted by the Kansas City Royals while still at

Dan Marino, at age three, riding his favorite rocking horse.

Marino wore number 14 when he started for his freshman high school football team.

Central Catholic High School. As a pitcher, he compiled a 25-1 record in his final two seasons there; he also hit over .500. The Royals offered him a contract to sign and report to the minor leagues.

"I was thrilled," Marino says. "It also meant a very tough decision, one of the toughest I've ever had to make. Would it be baseball or football?"

What made it such a hard decision was Marino's skills in football. He was a *Parade Magazine* All-American at quarterback, and nearly every major college in the nation wanted him. Many of the great football programs were offering a free college education if only Marino would play for them.

"It was very tempting to take the Royals' offer and the chance to go right into professional baseball," Marino says. "But I said no. I had all of these college offers to play football and receive a scholarship. I wanted the college education . . . I couldn't see throwing away college for football or baseball."

The decision to play football had been tough. Now came another tough decision. Which college would win his services? Marino was impressed by what he knew of UCLA and the University of Miami.

But there was one thing neither school could offer him. Dan loved playing before his friends and family. That feeling went back to the fifth grade at St. Regis Elementary School, where Dan and his teammates attended mass on Sunday mornings in their football uniforms. Then they'd march behind cheerleaders down the middle of the street to the field. Only one school offered him the chance to stay near home: The University of Pittsburgh.

"Pitt was the perfect situation," Marino says. "I could play in the city I grew up in. Everybody knew me. Although I'd be living in a dorm, any time I wanted to, I could go home for dinner and see my family. I could round up the guys for a pickup game. Everything I needed was right there."

Pickup games had always been important to Dan. As a kid, hardly a day went by without him going out on the ballfields or courts, throwing passes or pitches, dribbling, or rebounding. Marino has never won a championship in football—not in Pop Warner, high school, college, or with the Dolphins. In his pickup games, he could always be a champ.

"We were all going to be these great pro stars," says Bill Sabo, one of Marino's childhood buddies. "We'd be out playing all the time, and when Dan went to Pitt, we still would get together to play ball."

Dan and his friends often played on the streets of Oakland. Those were some of the most intense games he's ever been a part of. "There weren't very many fields around my house, so we used to play football in the street," he says. "You could only have three or four guys on a team because the street was so narrow and we'd use telephone poles for end zones. The curbs were out of bounds.

"Some of the throws were down hill. It was

more competitive playing in neighborhood games than many other games."

The pickup games were great training for Dan. "I was always playing against older kids. I think that helped me a lot. Older guys were picking me to be the quarterback."

The greater Pittsburgh area has been the breeding ground of many great football players. Joe Namath, Joe Montana, Mike Ditka, Tony Dorsett, and numerous other Hall of Famers grew up there. Dan Marino had different football heroes: the Pittsburgh Steelers.

"I was a big Steelers fan, of course, when I was growing up. In the street, I would pretend that I was in the middle of Three Rivers Stadium instead."

Those were the championship days, when the Steel Curtain crushed opposing offenses, when Terry Bradshaw, Franco Harris, Lynn Swann, and John Stallworth destroyed opposing defenses. The Steelers won four Super Bowls in six years when Marino was growing up, and he imagined that someday he would lead them to many more titles.

"Our Sunday morning games were never enough," he remembers. "When the Steelers were on TV, we'd watch the first half, and then at halftime we'd run outside and have another quick game."

Marino and his friends also played games such as street hockey, often in the schoolyard where broken windows sometimes ended the game. "They chased us out of there when that happened," Marino says.

The games weren't always friendly. One day, Sabo and Marino got into a fight and Sabo gave his buddy a black eye. "My first," Marino recalls.

"We had just got done playing a game and he said he was thirsty," Sabo says. "I was, too. He tried to get in line ahead of me. I wasn't going to just give in to him."

Not that Marino ever expected people to hand him anything. Not with Dan Marino, Sr., who drove a delivery truck, showing the way. "My dad taught me that you work for everything," Dan says. "I learned that as a kid and I never forgot it."

On the football field, Marino was not just a passer but a good runner, too. In one game against St. Regis's main rival, St. Philomena, Dan scored all of his team's touchdowns. Not bad for a guy who had once served as the team's water boy because he was too young to play for it.

After college, Marino would go off to star for Miami. But the neighborhood has never forgotten him. The field where he played so often, overlooking the old neighborhood and the Monongahela River, has been named Dan Marino Field.

3

DAN THE PANTHER

Dan Marino never won a high school championship because he did not have enough excellent teammates. But the University of Pittsburgh had fielded a number of top-notch athletes, and boosters of the team were looking forward to the Panthers winning a national title.

As a freshman, Marino played behind Rick Trocano. Few freshmen get to start at quarterback, but many of Dan's teammates—impressed by his cannon arm and pro style—felt it would not be long before he would take over.

Trocano was hurt in midseason and Marino started the seventh game, against Navy. He led the team to five straight victories. Pitt wound up 11-1, ranked number seven in the nation. In the Fiesta Bowl, Marino led the Panthers to a victory over the University of Arizona. Dan ended the season with 1,680 yards passing, a Pitt fresh-

Dan Marino made his first collegiate start at quarterback in his rookie season. He threw for two touchdowns as the University of Pittsburgh beat Syracuse University 28–21.

Marino had a fine sophomore season in college until he suffered a knee injury. Here he is sacked by Boston College's Junior Poles.

man record.

A knee injury shortened his sophomore year, but Dan still threw for 1,513 yards and 14 touchdowns. Again Pitt finished 11-1. The University of Georgia was ranked number one in the nation; Pitt was ranked number two.

By the time he was 20 and a junior, people were comparing Marino to another local product, John Unitas. They predicted Dan would win the Heisman Trophy, annually awarded to the top college football player.

"There's not a better quarterback in the country," Pitt coach Jackie Sherrill said. "He has talent, poise, intelligence, confidence, everything you want in your quarterback and your leader.

"He also wants the ball in his hands in close games. Danny thinks he can't be stopped and the other guys start thinking that way, too."

The Panthers were thinking national championship in 1981. They had lost only one game in each of their previous two seasons and clearly had one of the best teams in the country.

Pitt eased through its first six games, allowing no more than 14 points in five of those wins, scoring at least 26 in four of them. "We really were rolling, on offense and defense," Marino said. "We felt like we could beat anyone and that we deserved to be number one."

After a 29–24 win over Boston College—one of the rare so-so performances by the Panthers— Pitt was anointed as the number one team in the polls. Pitt then romped through the easiest part of the schedule, destroying Rutgers University, 47–3; Army, 48–0; and Temple University, 35–0.

Pitt headed into its yearly meeting with Penn State University, its top rival, ranked atop the polls. Marino and company were dreaming of an unbeaten regular season, something Pitt had not done since it won the national championship at 12-0 in 1976.

Penn State came into the game with an 8-2 record, ranked 11th. Its losses had come to the powerful universities of Miami and Alabama. It had lost in 1979 and 1980 to the Panthers and wanted nothing more than to erase the bitter memory of those defeats by ending Pitt's run at the top.

The city of Pittsburgh was alive with football fever. In normal years, the Pitt–Penn State game is a big deal. When one of the teams is heading for a national title, the rivalry becomes the biggest story in the state.

"Everywhere you went, on campus and in the city, there was excitement over the game," Dan said. "People would come up to you and say that they thought it was the biggest thing to happen in Pittsburgh, along with the Steelers. This is a great football town, and it was great the way people were talking about us."

Marino kept the excitement high by leading the Panthers to touchdowns the first two times they had the ball. They were flying high, ready to continue their streak of one-sided wins.

But the Nittany Lions clamped down. They kept the Panthers from scoring again. Pitt's defense let down for the first time all season. Final score: Penn State 48, Pitt 14.

Good-bye number one ranking. Good-bye national championship.

"I started crying with about eight minutes to go in the game," said Cindi Marino, Dan's sister, who also went to Pitt. "I just sat there and couldn't stop crying.

"Then I looked around and saw that so many people had left. They were fair-weather fans. So I got mad. I stood up and started cheering."

She was about the only one. Many fans had booed Marino and the Panthers, forgetting all the team had done during the season. Dan senior knew his son heard the boos. He also knew Danny could handle it. "He understands you're not going to make everyone happy," Dan senior said. "And he knows you can't win all the time. So you learn to deal with it."

"After a loss like the one to Penn State," Danny said, "it's nice to have a family so close. It helped to come home and talk to my dad and my family and know they still love me."

The Sugar Bowl could have been the final step to a national title, but the upset by Penn State took care of that. Dan was determined not to let the season end on such a sour note.

Pitt's opponent was the University of Georgia, featuring superstar running back Herschel Walker. Walker had lifted the Bulldogs to a national title as a freshman in 1980, edging the Panthers in the polls. New Orleans, Louisiana, the site of the Sugar Bowl, was close enough for thousands of fans to make the trip from Georgia; few Panthers fans would be found in the stands of the Superdome.

Georgia fought to gain a 20–17 lead, but that

would not be enough. Marino got the ball at his 20 with 3:46 remaining in the game. He led the Panthers to the Georgia 33 yardline with his passing and an 8-yard run. Then, spotting a zone defense, he looked for tight end John Brown down the middle. As the clock ticked down to 35 seconds left, Marino hit Brown perfectly for the winning score. In all, Dan completed 26 of 41 passes for 261 yards and three touchdowns. It was the first of dozens of great comebacks led by Marino.

"That's a pass I will remember all my life," he says. "What a great way to end a season."

In 1981, Marino threw for 37 touchdowns and 2,876 yards. He finished fourth in the Heisman voting, and became the school's all-time leading passer.

Dan's senior year wasn't nearly as memorable. He did wind up setting 13 school records and he took the Panthers to the Cotton Bowl. But under new coach Foge Fazio they were only 9-3. Most schools would be very happy with a 9-3 record, but for Marino and the Panthers, it was a letdown.

Dan's numbers weren't as good his senior year. He struggled, and the fans let him have it. Sitting in the stands at Pitt Stadium, Dan's mom didn't always hear what she wanted to

John Brown (left) and Dan Marino celebrate after hooking up on the winning touchdown in the 1982 Sugar Bowl. The 33-yard pass came with only 35 seconds left in the game.

hear. In fact, there were games when she wanted to scream at the fans who didn't like the way her son was playing or how the Panthers were doing.

"Inside, I'm just grinding," Victoria Marino would say. "Some of the things they say . . . you can't imagine. I wouldn't want to hear such things about anyone, and they are saying them about my son."

Dan senior laughed at his wife's comments. "I don't look at Danny as a kid any more. He can handle himself. He's a big boy now."

Marino's dad got "a big kick" out of the radio call-in shows, even if his son was taking a beating from the callers. "It will help him be a man," Dan senior said. "You'll never please everyone, and you have to learn to take that stuff. There's always somebody who wants to know why you didn't do this or that, why you didn't pass to this guy or run on that down. I think Dan knows how to handle that."

The University of Pittsburgh knew how to handle Marino's greatness. After his senior season, it retired his number 13 jersey.

"The University of Pittsburgh is very proud of you, Danny, as an athlete and as a young man," athletic director Ed Bozik said after Marino joined Tony Dorsett and Hugh Green in being honored with a retired number. "Never again will another Pitt football player wear the number 13 jersey. It will be retired in our locker room."

Praise came from everywhere.

"The show Dan Marino put on against us in the Sugar Bowl is one of the greatest ever," Georgia coach Vince Dooley said.

"Dan Marino is the best quarterback I've ever coached against at the collegiate level,"

Penn State coach Joe Paterno added.

Overall, the Pitt experience was a good one for Dan. He never won a national championship, and he did slip to 27th in the first round of the 1983 draft. But that draft became famous for the quality of the quarterbacks taken in the first round: John Elway, Todd Blackledge, Jim Kelly, Tony Eason, and Ken O'Brien all quickly became starters for their teams. The best quarterback of all was the sixth taken.

"That was disappointing, because I felt I had as good a career in college as anybody," Marino said. "Then, pick after pick and I'm not taken, and five other quarterbacks go. But it worked out pretty well, didn't it?"

Marino's choice to go to Pitt worked out pretty well, too. "I made a good decision," he said. "It's great to be able to play in front of my friends and my family. I played a lot and I couldn't have played any more anyplace else. I was home, I got great publicity. I'm a hometown boy."

4

DAN THE RECORD SETTER

Dan Marino was disappointed with the way the NFL draft worked out for a number of reasons. His first wish was for the Steelers to pick him, but they seemed settled on Mark Malone. He had hoped to be the first quarterback drafted, but of course that did not happen either.

When the Dolphins made Dan their first choice, he knew that he was going to play for one of the greatest coaches and teachers in pro football history, Don Shula.

"During my first meeting with coach Shula, he said he felt I was good enough to help the team now, not down the road," Marino said. "He said that I should come in and be ready to compete for the starting job right away. He didn't care how old I was. He would judge me on what I could do for the Dolphins."

When Dan Marino leaped into the pro ranks, he was disappointed only to be the sixth quarterback taken in the 1983 draft. In training camp, he soon showed the Dolphins how brilliant they had been in selecting him.

David Woodley (left) was the veteran quarterback who had led the Dolphins to the Super Bowl. But his days were numbered after Marino joined the team.

In January 1992, Miami played the Super Bowl. Three months later, they drafted Marino. David Woodley was the starting quarterback, a good scrambler and leader, but not much of a passer. The Dolphins had the NFL's worst passing rating that year.

Woodley probably realized his days were numbered as the number one quarterback in Miami when Dan signed a four-year contract for nearly $2 million. "I didn't think I would start right away, but I did think I would start soon," Marino said.

Rather than take a free trip to Italy during the summer, Dan stayed home and got ready for training camp. He did well in exhibition games, but so did Woodley, and Shula owed Woodley the opportunity to prove he could keep up his winning ways.

Woodley kept his starter's status when the season opened, but Dan got into several games. Against the Raiders—who would go on to win the Super Bowl that year—Marino threw two touchdown passes.

By the sixth game, Shula had seen enough. Woodley could only take the Dolphins so far, and that was not far enough. "The time has come," he told his rookie, "the job is yours. I know you can do the job. That's why we drafted you and that's what you expect from yourself."

Miami's next opponent was the Buffalo Bills. The Bills jumped out to a 14–0 lead as Dan made what he called "careless mistakes. I was too anxious to make a big play."

Marino recovered his poise. He threw for 268 yards and three touchdowns, giving the Dolphins the lead. But the Bills rallied and won in overtime.

All anyone could talk about after the game was Dan Marino.

"That kid is a winner," said Miami center Dwight Stephenson. "That's just the first."

"He showed what he's going to do in this league, and that's just to rip it apart," added star receiver Nat Moore.

Moore was exactly correct. The Dolphins won nine of their last 11 games to win the AFC East. That included a win over the San Francisco 49ers after Joe Montana injured his thigh in the second half. Marino and Montana would meet again on a bigger stage.

The end of Marino's season was spoiled by problems with his knees. He missed two games, and knee problems would become a continual worry throughout the rest of his career. If he had stayed healthy in 1983, Marino would have set a record for most touchdown passes by a rookie. He finished with 20, two short of the mark.

Still, Marino did lead the AFC in passing with a 96.0 rating, the first rookie ever to do so. He was also the first rookie quarterback named to start the Pro Bowl, football's equivalent of the All-Star Game. In starting the Pro Bowl, he beat out such luminaries as Dan Fouts, Jim Plunkett, and Ken Anderson.

"That has been one of the greatest honors

I've received," Marino said. "To be a rookie and to be playing with all these great players."

In the following year, all those great players were honored to be on the same field as Marino.

In 1984, his second NFL season, Marino was a true magician. He might have been satisfied with merely improving a bit on his fine rookie season. Instead, he had the best passing season any quarterback has ever had.

In the first game of the year, against the defending NFC champion, the Washington Redskins, Marino got off to a fast start. Despite a preseason finger injury, Marino threw for 311 yards and 5 touchdowns. It was a sign of things to come as the Dolphins romped, 35–17.

"He keeps rising to the occasion," coach Don Shula said. "The important thing is he's not afraid to let go. If the defense makes a good play on him, he doesn't go into a shell."

Marino passed for two more touchdowns in the second game, a win over New England, and three more in a victory at Buffalo. Then came two against the Indianapolis Colts and three against the St. Louis Cardinals. One reporter asked if a certain touchdown pass was easy.

"Who's to say what's easy and what isn't?" he asked. "I'm not the one who is making it look easy."

"It looked easy, but [receiver] Mark Duper had to read the blitz and I had to read the blitz. He had to know what to do—stutter step on the cornerback and then hit it. We've got to know what we're doing. Sometimes it works, sometimes it doesn't."

Everything was working, and the Dolphins were 5-0.

Marino made his first trip to Pittsburgh as a

pro and thrilled his family and friends, if not the rest of the Steelers fans, by picking apart what had been the Steel Curtain. He passed for two second-quarter touchdowns in a 31–7 win.

"I've always wondered what it would be like to play there as a pro," said Marino, admitting he usually dreamed of doing it as a Steeler. "I didn't really feel nervous, just anxious to play."

How did he feel afterward?

"As good as ever," he answered.

Against the Houston Oilers, Dan had three more touchdown passes, and he got four against New England as the Dolphins improved to 8-0. Halfway through the season, Marino had 24

In the 1984 season opener, Marino threw for five touchdowns in a 35–17 win.

touchdown passes. The league record was 36, held by George Blanda and Y. A. Tittle, both Hall of Fame quarterbacks.

"The guy is unstoppable," Cardinals quarterback Neil Lomax said after Marino set a team record with 429 yards through the air.

"It's hard to believe Dan is only in his second year, considering all the things he has accomplished," Shula said. "He deserves all the recognition that he can get. He's done things that nobody else has done. But what's so great about him is the way that he does it, in a way that you don't even notice it while he does it."

Typically, Dan refused to take credit for his amazing season. Instead, he praised others. "You have to look at the offensive line to understand why we could get so many [touchdowns]," he said. "When you get as much time as they gave me, you should be able to find people open. And when you aren't getting hit when you throw, you can get the ball just where you want it.

"We have a very intelligent offensive line that doesn't make many errors," he continued. "No quarterback can do well without getting that kind of help. I'm kind of shocked when I'm sacked, because those guys are so good on the line."

The Dolphins had been so good for half a season that people were wondering if they could match the 1972 Dolphins, the only NFL team ever to win every regular season game and every playoff game, including the Super Bowl. That team had featured receiver Paul Warfield, running backs Jim Kiick and Larry Csonka, and quarterback Bob Griese. Griese had become a legend in Miami; when he retired, many fans felt they would never see his likes again. All subsequent Miami quarterbacks were compared to Griese and found wanting. All, that is, until Marino.

In the ninth game, the Dolphins romped over Buffalo, 38–7; Marino threw for three more touchdowns. The next week, they went to 10-0 by defeating the New York Jets, 31–17. Dan had two more touchdown passes.

"The guy is unstoppable," Jets defensive end Mark Gastineau said. "You get near him and he gets off his pass, and darn if it doesn't go for a big gain. And they make sure you don't get near him very much."

Coach Shula had always thought Miami's perfect 1972 season couldn't be equaled. But he was beginning to think that just maybe this team might do it. "We've really been on a great roll, making all of the plays we need," he said as the Dolphins got ready to play a home game against the Philadelphia Eagles. "To win every game, you have to get everyone pitching in, you have to be a bit lucky, and, mostly, you have to stay healthy. What has amazed me is we've

Marino was not the only person setting records in 1984. Mark Clayton established a record by catching 18 of Marino's touchdown throws.

Don Shula congratulates his quarterback in the closing seconds of the Dolphin's win over the Pittsburgh Steelers in the 1985 AFC championship game.

hardly had a close game."

That soon changed. Philadelphia roared off to a 14–0 lead as Ron Jaworski hit two touchdown passes in the first quarter. It was the first time Miami did not score first in a game all year.

Just before halftime, Marino took the Dolphins 76 yards for a touchdown. His 11-yard pass to Tony Nathan would make it 14–7 and be Dan's only touchdown toss of the game; it was the only time all season he did not have at least two scoring passes.

The Eagles got a field goal in the third quarter. Miami answered as Woody Bennett and Pete Johnson had touchdown runs after Dan got the team in scoring position. When Uwe von Schamann kicked a 27-yard field goal, Miami had a 24–17 lead.

Jaworski was not through, however. He led Philadelphia on a long drive. Mel Hoover caught a 38-yard touchdown pass. Then came the kind of play that sparks teams to reach the most difficult goals. Doug Betters, the Dolphins 6'7" defensive end, leaped up and blocked the extra point. Miami held on to win by a point.

"What was that I said about not having close games?" Shula said after the tight win. "Forget that."

A week later, it was time to forget the unbeaten season.

Miami, which had not lost a regular-season game in more than a year, blew a 14-point lead in the fourth quarter. The San Diego Chargers' Dan Fouts, headed for the Hall of Fame, threw for two of his four touchdowns on the day. The second pass capped a 91-yard drive that tied the game.

Marino once again got the Dolphins close enough to win the game, but von Schamann missed a 44-yard field goal as time expired.

In overtime, Miami never got a chance. San Diego won the coin toss and Fouts, like Marino a master late in games, drove them to the win. Buford McGee ran 25 yards for the score that ended the Dolphins' streak.

"I don't think any of us really were planning on going 16-0," Marino said. "We just want to win the division and be in a position to get to the Super Bowl. We don't need to be 16-0 to do that."

But it sure would have been nice, right Dan?

"Yeah," he said with a smile. "Something like that always is nice to think about, but it almost never happens."

Miami got back on the right track the next week, beating the Jets, 28–17, as Dan put all four touchdowns on the scoreboard. He hit Bruce Hardy twice and Mark Clayton and Dan Johnson once each for scores. That gave Marino 36 touchdown passes in 13 games, tying the league record. Blanda and Tittle each had taken 14 games to set the record.

Dan was not thinking very much about setting the record, though. "If it comes, it comes," he said. "I kind of believe I'll throw another one in the next three games."

He didn't wait long at all to set the mark. In

the game against the Raiders, he first threw a pass that went for a 97-yard touchdown—for the wrong team. Mike Haynes picked off the rare Marino interception and dashed the length of the field to put his team ahead.

But moments after that, Marino led his team down to the Raiders' 4 yardline. For his historic touchdown, Marino turned to a veteran, Jimmy Cefalo. His 37th touchdown put him in the record books.

Dan threw for three more touchdowns that day and set a team record with 470 passing yards. As Miami's defense fell apart, a desperate Marino put the ball in the air 57 times, completing 35. But it wasn't enough. The Raiders won, 45–34. The Dolphins now had lost twice in three games.

"I don't want to pass that much in a game," Marino said. I'd rather throw 20 times and be in control of the game instead of being forced to throw and throw."

Miami got back to its winning ways with a victory over Indianapolis as Dan continued his unreal streak with four more touchdown passes. That gave him 44 for the season.

As if he wanted to push the record beyond anyone's reach, Dan threw for four more in the final game on the schedule, a Monday night win over the Dallas Cowboys. Marino hit Clayton with a 63-yarder to win the game in the final minutes. The Dolphins ended with a superb 14-2 record and Marino ended with an unreal 48 touchdowns.

"I don't think you can dream up a better year than Dan has had," Clayton said. "It's like he feels he can throw a touchdown from anywhere, in any situation. And we feel like if we get just a little room . . . boom, it's a touch-down."

Heading into the playoffs as the AFC's best team, the Dolphins had ridden Marino's arm to their best record since their Super Bowl season. Dan set five NFL passing marks with 362 completions for 5,084 yards (the first time any quarterback had passed the 5,000-yard marker), 48 touchdowns, and nine games with over 300 yards passing and four over 400 yards.

Dan averaged nearly 318 yards passing a game. In 1981, Dan Fouts had 360 completions and 4,802 yards in the air. Now those records were Marino's.

Marino was sacked only 13 times the whole season. Mark Clayton caught 18 touchdown passes, then an NFL record. (Jerry Rice of the San Francisco 49ers would break that record in 1987.)

Marino was given the NFL offensive player of the year award and most valuable player honors. In almost any other year, Eric Dickerson of the Los Angeles Rams would have won both titles as he rushed for a record 2,105 yards. But Marino won those honors hands down, taking in all nine different MVP trophies.

"It's something special, because there are so many great players in the league," Marino said. "It's nice to have all the records. But it's better to play on a team that can win as many games as this one has.

"I think I'm fortunate, because I've been able to play with great players to help me accomplish a lot of good things," Marino continued. "Any award I get makes me feel good, because it shows the guys were able to help me out."

Next, they had to help him out in the playoffs.

First came the Seattle Seahawks, the team that had knocked the Dolphins out of the play-offs in 1983. Marino threw for three touchdowns and the Dolphins shut out the Seahawks in the second half to post a 31–10 win.

Next came another meeting with the Steelers, this time in Miami. For the Marino clan, it was a strange feeling.

"My whole family grew up rooting for the Steelers," Dan said. "There never was another team for us, and then, here I am, leading the Dolphins against the Steelers for the chance to go to the Super Bowl."

Not that any of Dan's friends or relatives had any doubt about whom to root for: Dolphins all the way.

And that's how the game turned out. Marino hit four lightning-quick touchdowns, giving him 55 in 18 games. The drives for those four scores totaled 5 minutes, 42 seconds. He passed for 421 yards. Miami won 45–28.

Dan Marino, in his second NFL season, was going to the Super Bowl.

"We should give Danny a game ball for every game," defensive back Glenn Blackwood said.

"With Dan Marino throwing the ball," Tony Nathan added, "we feel like we can do anything."

The biggest test was next. San Francisco rolled over their opponents all year long, winning 15 and losing only one time. They became the first NFL team ever to win 15 games during the regular season. The 49ers' Joe Montana had established a reputation as a great quarterback, earning the nickname "The Comeback Kid" for his frequent last-minute heroics.

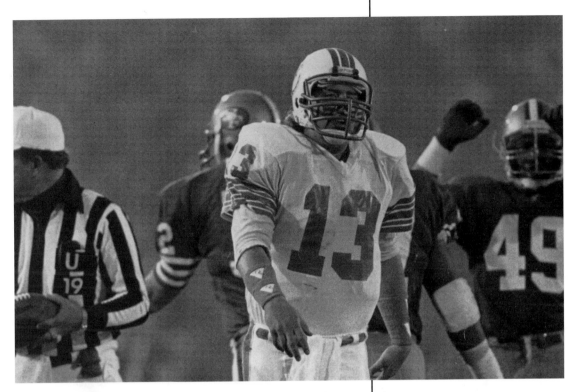

Many writers and broadcasters hyped the showdown between the two best slingers in the NFL, forgetting that no one player can win a game all by himself. When game time finally arrived, Marino and Montana both showed their stuff. But it was the 49ers' defense that proved they were the best, as San Francisco won their second of a record five Super Bowls.

Montana refused to let the game be turned into a passing circus. "I think the biggest thing for me was knowing the type of passer [Marino] is," Montana said. "I could not get caught up in that type of game and let myself get pulled away from the game plan. I just had to let our offense work as it normally did, and if they scored a touchdown, not say, 'We've got to get one back right away.'"

Marino walks back to the bench in the 1985 Super Bowl. He had just been sacked by Jeff Fuller (right) of the San Francisco 49ers. The 49ers humbled the Dolphins, 38–16.

Ten days after the Super Bowl loss, Marino married Claire Veazey at St. Regis Church in Pittsburgh.

Montana won MVP honors. He completed 24 of 35 passes for 331 yards and three touchdowns, as the 49ers romped, 38–16. Montana set Super Bowl records for most passing yards, most rushing yards by a quarterback (59), and most pass attempts without an interception.

Meantime, Marino was sacked four times, the most in any game all season. The 49ers switched from a three-man defensive line to a four-man line with six or seven backs in order to confuse Marino. Even when Marino had time to look downfield, his receivers were covered.

Marino attempted 50 passes and gained 318 yards in the air, but he was also intercepted twice. San Francisco's coach, Bill Walsh, had put together a perfect game plan.

"Dan Marino is a great young quarterback," Walsh said. "But in my mind, Joe Montana is the best quarterback in the game today and maybe of all time. Marino will have his day, but this was Joe Montana's day."

Marino was left wondering what happened. At 23 years of age, he was the youngest quarterback ever to start a Super Bowl. But he never has gotten back to the big game, never had the chance Walsh predicted for him.

"Maybe we were happy just to be there, happy to be playing in the Super Bowl," Dan said. "I'm sure no one will ever forget what we did in 1984. It was a super season; we did some things that haven't been done in a long, long time. But I'd trade every record we broke to be Super Bowl champions."

5

DAN THE ALL-PRO

For eight seasons, Dan Marino was the Dolphins player defenders feared and respected the most. They saw how he could pick apart other teams, and they knew he could do it to their team, too.

The Dolphins were not especially good in many of the years between 1985 and 1992. Not once did they make the Super Bowl. Only in three of those years—1985, 1990, and 1992—were they in the playoffs.

Despite making five Pro Bowls in that span and collecting most of his record 15 AFC player of the week awards, Dan could not lift the Dolphins to the top.

No one blamed him. Miami's defense was weak, at one point falling near the bottom of the league in yardage allowed. Teams found they could run on the Dolphins, which kept Marino and the offense off the field.

"You want to get out there and do things,

Marino grimaces in pain after he tore his Achilles tendon in a 1993 game against the Cleveland Browns.

but sometimes it doesn't work out that way," Dan said. "The other teams are trying to find ways to beat you, too."

Often they found those ways by avoiding shootouts. Marino has thrown for four touchdowns or more in 19 games; only four of those games were losses. So other teams have labored to shut down the pass, using as many as six or seven defensive backs. In effect, they dare the Dolphins to beat them win the run, something Miami has rarely been able to do.

"For a few years," said Mark Clayton, who has caught more passes (538) and more touchdowns (79) than any other Dolphin, "we knew if we could make a game wide-open, we could win. We felt nobody could match us at quarterback."

But while Marino was piling up great passing numbers and setting records, other quarterbacks from the 1983 draft were getting to the big game.

John Elway, the first pick in that draft, got the Denver Broncos to three Super Bowls. Then Jim Kelly took the Bills to four in a row. Tony Eason also got to one with New England. Curiously, the record of these four fine quarterbacks is 0-9 in the Super Bowl.

Marino has won a fine percentage of his regular season games—at the end of 1994, his career record was 107-63, a .630 winning percentage. But in the heart of his career, he and the Dolphins were 73-54, a .575 winning percentage. Worse, when they got into the playoffs, they put together only a record of 3-3, hardly good enough to win championships.

Yet nobody will say that Dan wasn't a great quarterback in those years. In fact, trying to keep a so-so team in the playoff race might have been the toughest chore of his career.

"I've never been hung up on my personal statistics," he said. "What counts to me is winning. The only stat I am really interested in is the number of victories we have at the end of the year.

"My goals each season are to help my team win every single game, especially the last one in January, and to play the best and the hardest that I possibly can," he continued. "To me, consistency is the key to being a great player."

How consistent was Marino in the middle of his career? Check out these facts.

Only in 1988, when Miami was 6-10, the worst record of any season in the Marino Era, did the Dolphins not score at least 331 points.

Only in 1990 did Marino throw for fewer than 3,876 yards, and the team was 12-4 that year. That same season, Miami was fifth in overall passing, its lowest ranking from 1985–1992. The Dolphins ranked first in NFL passing three times and were second twice.

In every season of his career, Marino has thrown more touchdowns than interceptions. In the 1985–1992 span, he had 222 touchdown passes and 142 interceptions.

In 1986, Marino's busiest passing season, he threw 623 times, completing 378, both career highs. With all those passes, Dan had his sec-

Marino's injury forced him to watch the rest of the 1993 season from the sidelines.

ond-highest completion percentage (60.7) and third-highest passer rating (92.5).

Of the 15 highest-passing-yardage seasons in league history, Marino's name appears five times. Four of those seasons came between his only Super Bowl and his Achilles tendon injury.

Perhaps Marino's greatest strength at quarterback is his ability to stage late-game rallies. "With Marino at quarterback, the Dolphins never are out of a game," Bills linebacker Darryl Talley said. "I've been playing against the guy forever, and you always wonder what he can do next. But he finds something. Our guy (Jim Kelly) has that talent too. Marino has done it so many times, he must believe he can do it every time the Dolphins are behind."

That's exactly what Marino thinks. "If there's still time on the clock, you're still in the game," he says.

Here's how consistent Dan is: he rallied the Dolphins from behind in the fourth quarter to win at least once in every pro season, including an amazing six times in 1992.

While Dan was succeeding on the field, he also grew in other ways. He began the Dan Marino Foundation to help children with problems in south Florida. He became involved in charity work for other causes, thinking nothing of flying across the country to appear in a golf tournament to aid the less fortunate.

Dan and his wife have three sons and a daughter. Their second oldest child, Michael, was diagnosed as being somewhat autistic at age 2½. He goes to a special school and Dan has become very active in helping research autism.

"He's doing real good. It could be a lot worse," Dan said. "It's something he'll have his whole life. But we caught it at an early age and we've been able to help him with schools. I think I'm pretty lucky in a lot of ways. Michael is a beautiful kid, very loving and social. There's a lot of people in a lot of tougher situations."

6

THE INJURY AND THE COMEBACK

It was a normal play Dan Marino had done thousands of times in his career. He dropped back to pass on the grass at Cleveland Stadium and made a short throw over the middle to Terry Kirby for a 10-yard gain.

However, at the end of it, even though he was not hit, Marino fell to the ground. The Achilles tendon in his right heel had snapped. "I didn't really know what happened," he said. "I heard a pop and then I was down and felt this awful pain. It felt like I had been shot."

There were no Browns or Dolphins near him. He had not been kicked in the heel. His foot was not stepped on. He had not put his leg into a hole. It did not make sense.

Marino, perhaps the greatest passer in NFL history, had also set a record for being the most healthy. He had started 145 straight games, something no other quarterback had ever done.

After Marino had his great game against the Patriots, he had a poor outing against the Buffalo Bills. Here Phil Hanson (number 90) bats down a pass attempt.

At times, Dan suffered knee injuries. He played with them. He needed minor surgery to fix his left knee five times, each time after the season was over. He compared that to changing the oil in a car.

Marino had missed three games during the 1987 players strike, but was the only quarterback to start every game since then. Counting playoff games, Marino played in 155 games in a row. He kept extending the streak even though Miami's offensive line, once a stone wall around Marino, no longer was so strong. In recent seasons, Dan got hit and knocked down more and more. Yet the 145 straight starts were 29 more than the next best total, set by Ron Jaworski of Philadelphia (1977–1984). Marino seemed to be the indestructible quarterback.

It took Marino a little time to realize his streak was over. He told team doctor Dan Kanell to "help me up and I'll be all right." The doctor looked down at the fallen Marino and told him, "Sorry, but no way."

Dan cried.

"You don't know how to react to something like that," Marino said later. "You play the game all your life, then it is taken away. It's a wake-up call. I went for so many years not even thinking about missing a game. I love to play football; it has been my whole life. And I never was on the sidelines, watching other guys play. Then you get an injury and it all is taken away from you. It hurts."

The worst part, Marino admits, was watching the Dolphins fall apart at the end of the 1993 season. By Thanksgiving, with untested Scott Mitchell playing well at quarterback, Miami did not miss a beat. After a wild holiday win in the snow at Dallas, the Dolphins stood atop the entire NFL. But injuries to a dozen key players after Marino had gone down ruined their season. They lost their last five games after a 9-2 start and didn't make the playoffs.

"I couldn't help, and that bothered me the most," Marino said. "Nothing is tougher on an athlete than standing there and not being a part of what you've been a big part of for so long. You want to be the one out there throwing the ball, making the decisions, win or lose. Especially win. But I also learned you have to enjoy every minute you play, no matter if you are in your second year or your 12th. It all goes by so fast. It doesn't really last very long."

The recovery from the injury did take a long time. Dan dedicated himself to making every minute count toward getting back on the field at the start of the 1994 schedule. He spent "more hours than I care to remember" working his way back: doing leg lifts, stretching, swimming, treadmill walks, biking. He even lifted weights, something he had not done since before he was an NFL star, and something few quarterbacks did until recent years.

Marino began yoga classes to be strong of mind and more graceful of body; he now can bend over and touch the floor without bending his knees, something he could not remember ever doing as a Dolphin. The yoga helped improve his concentration and helped him stay relaxed and prepared even when faced with hard decisions or tough times.

The heel injury, which made him use crutches for weeks—did not prevent him from throwing a ball. At age 33, he was sure the arm strength still would be there, "but I wasn't going to get lazy about it." So Marino threw and threw and threw. Anyone willing to play catch with him was fine with Dan. He made sure he could rely on his arm.

Marino also made sure he stayed around the Dolphins during the 1993 season. He helped his replacements, Scott Mitchell, Doug Pederson, and Steve DeBerg, with the game plans. "I give Dan tremendous credit for myself being able to play as quickly as I have been able to," said the veteran DeBerg, who became a starter one week after joining the team as a free agent. "He's helped me a lot. He sits next to me in meetings and explains the offense and his ideas on attacking the defense."

Dan refused to let his injury bother him psychologically. "Actually, I was kind of surprised," DeBerg said. "I wasn't sure how he would react in that situation. He had such high hopes for this year, and I'm sure he's disappointed that he's not the quarterback out there."

That was 1993. By the summer of 1994, Marino was back at his position. But he didn't have the backing of everyone. He still had discomfort in his foot and completed just 13 of 31 passes for 164 yards in the final two preseason games, both losses. Veteran Bernie Kosar, his new backup and still a hero in Florida from the days when he played for the University of Miami, did well in exhibitions. Fans were calling for Kosar to start the season as late as the week before the season opener.

"I was just a little sluggish," Marino said. "I think the whole offense was. But we weren't playing at the same pace as if we were playing against the New England Patriots on Sunday. This week is the time it counts, and I've been looking forward to it since last year, when I got hurt."

Marino erased so much of the hurt with the game of his life. He knew he could stop worrying about his heel. It would never be perfect, but he knew he still could do great things.

And he knew that the Dolphins finally had gotten better on defense, maybe even good enough to beat out the Buffalo Bills in the AFC East, stopping Buffalo's run of four straight Super Bowl appearances.

"I like the makeup of this team," Marino said early in the season, when the Dolphins were 3-0. "I think if we can avoid the injuries we had last year and keep everybody on the field, we can play with anyone."

Marino has been the one Dolphin who could play with—and outplay—anyone. On his way to the Hall of Fame, he has:

. led the Dolphins from behind in the fourth quarter to a victory 29 times

. made the Pro Bowl eight times

. set the record for most straight starts by a quarterback: 145

. had 11 years with at least 20 touchdown passes

. thrown 300 touchdown passes more quickly than anyone else: 157 games (second best was Fran Tarkenton: 217 games)

. thrown for 3,000 or more yards passing in 10 seasons (two more than Joe Montana)

. thrown for 3,000 or more yards nine seasons in a row—another record

. led the NFL in passing yardage five times, tying Sonny Jurgensen's mark.

Riding a high after the win over the Patriots, the Dolphins won at Green Bay as Marino com-

Trick play works! Marino celebrates with cornerback Sean Hill after Dan had fooled the New York Jets into thinking he was trying to stop the clock. Instead, Marino threw a winning touchdown pass to Mark Ingram.

pleted 17 of 25 passes, two for touchdowns and with no interceptions. The next week, against another 2-0 team, the Jets, Dan was even better. He hit on 23 of 31 passes for 289 yards and 2 touchdowns.

"Just a great game by one of the greatest quarterbacks ever," Jets safety Ronnie Lott said. "Dan showed he still has the touch."

That touch rarely would leave him during his comeback season. Miami lost 38–35 to the Minnesota Vikings, but Marino nearly blew the lid off the Metrodome in leading a rally from a 28–0 hole. He threw for 3 touchdowns and 430 yards, but he also was intercepted three times and on several occasions walked to the sidelines yelling at his teammates or himself.

The next week's game at Cincinnati normally would not have gotten much attention. But it was a matchup of Dolphins coach Don Shula and his son, Bengals coach David Shula. It was the first time father and son head coaches went against each other.

Dan knew how much it meant to his boss. "I wanted to make sure we gave him this one, sort of as a present for all he's done in his career," Marino said. "And we needed a win after the loss at Minnesota."

With a chance to prove they were ready to replace Buffalo as the division's top team, the Dolphins failed. They lost 21–11 and Dan had a poor game in high winds. Marino's mood didn't improve when he hit only 17 of 37 passes against the Raiders the next week. But at least Miami won in overtime, 20–17, when Marino directed them on a 10½-minute drive.

"There are games where it is a struggle, where I think about the heel," he said. "But I can't do that. It might never be the way it was, I know that. But I have to do my best with it to help this team."

That's just what Dan did in the rematch with Drew Bledsoe and the New England Patriots, a 23–3 win, and in a one-point victory over the Indianapolis Colts, when he succeeded on 30 of 41 passes.

But then came a loss to the Chicago Bears in which the running game didn't show up. And, in Game 11, Marino returned home to Pittsburgh, had a great meal, then a great game (31 for 45 for 312 yards and 1 touchdown). But the Dolphins lost again, 16–13 in overtime, and they dropped to 7-4.

"That was one of the most disappointing losses I've had," Marino said. "It was a great week, coming back to Pittsburgh, playing at Three Rivers Stadium. But it's not the way I wanted it to turn out. I don't know what it is, but we are not making as many plays as we should."

Then Marino made one of the best plays of his career, leading the Dolphins to a thrilling comeback win over the Jets on Thanksgiving weekend. Down 28–6, Marino threw three touchdown passes to Mark Ingram in the second half. On the last one, Marino faked spiking the ball at the Jets 8 yardline, making New York think he was most concerned about stopping the clock. As the Jets defense let up, Marino drew the ball back and fired a pass to Ingram in the corner of the end zone. It was a master stroke.

"If the defense doesn't go for the fake," Marino said, "you throw it out of bounds and still have time left."

"We messed up," Jets lineman Donald Evans said. "He made a real smart play and fooled us. That's what makes him such a winner."

Still, with a chance to break the AFC East wide open, the Dolphins failed. Buffalo beat them 42–31 at Joe Robbie Stadium as Dan threw four interceptions. He was mad. "I have to do better than that," he said.

So he did the next week against the Kansas City Chiefs to clinch a playoff spot. And he did in the season's final game, a win over the Detroit Lions that gave Miami the division title at 10-6.

The Dolphins first playoff opponent was the Kansas City Chiefs again. In the first game, Joe Montana, recently traded by San Francisco to the Chiefs, did not play as he was recuperating from a knee injury. This time, he would be back. It would be the first time Marino and Montana were on the same field since the 1985 Super Bowl.

"Danny is always excited," receiver O. J. McDuffie said, "but he was extra excited this week. I could tell that he was really pumped up. It carried over to the whole team."

In the first two periods of the playoff game, the quarterbacks combined to complete 26 of 31 passes for 340 yards. Montana hit 12 of 15, Marino 14 of 16. The score was tied, 17–17.

On the first series of the second half, in a perfect example of Marino's smarts, he spotted a blitz and found Irving Fryar for a touchdown. That would be enough as Miami won 27–17.

"That quarterback is special," Chiefs coach Marty Schottenheimer said. "He hasn't done what he's done with mirrors."

Next up were the Chargers as Marino's comeback closed in on the Super Bowl. In 1992, the Dolphins ended San Diego's quest for its first Super Bowl spot, routing the Chargers in the rain at Joe Robbie Stadium in the second round of the playoffs. The memory of that game made the Chargers twice as hungry to beat the Dolphins this time. But the long-ago memory of playing in a Super Bowl, something Dan had not been able to match, made Miami and its quarterback just as hungry.

"When you know you are getting closer to your goal, you just can't wait to get out on the field and get it done," Marino said. "The week goes by so slowly, because all you can think about and all people talk about and write about is the game, and that it's the next step to the Super Bowl. You can't wait to suit up and get it going."

At halftime of the game at San Diego, the Dolphins led 21–6. Marino had been unstoppable. "The way Dan was going,, I didn't know if

The rematch between Dan Marino and Joe Montana was a victory for the Dolphin great. Here he dives into the end zone despite the efforts of Chiefs safety William White.

we could catch up," Chargers All-Pro linebacker Junior Seau said.

San Diego found a way—by keeping the ball away from Marino. The Dolphins had it for only 7:22 of the second half and the Chargers rallied to go ahead 22–21. But Dan had 35 seconds left, which can be forever when you're trying to hold a thin lead.

"I thought we were dead, even after we scored," Chargers coach Bobby Ross said.

In 34 seconds, Marino brought the Dolphins to the Chargers 30 yardline. A deft mix of runs and bullet passes moved them up the field with the momentum of a cavalry charge. With one second on the clock, Pete Stoyanovich came out to try a very makeable 43-yard field goal. "That was Marino at his very best," Seau said.

Stoyanovich's kick missed wide right. Previously he had come through with big kicks and was reputed as one of the best kickers in the NFL. But now Marino had to head home, wondering if his last shot at an NFL title was gone.

"Any time you work the whole season and it ends like this, it's hard when you don't achieve your goal," he said. "It's tough."

But Marino promised to keep trying. "I've tried to cherish each moment of playing the game," he said. "You've been playing football since you were seven or eight years old, and there's going to be a time when that's going to stop. For me, it's hopefully not going to be for a long time, but you never know what's going to happen."

CHRONOLOGY

1961   Born in Pittsburgh, Pennsylvania, on September 15

1979   Offered minor league contract by Kansas City Royals; instead decides to accept scholarship from University of Pittsburgh to play football; sets record for most passing yards by a freshman

1981   Leads Panthers to third straight 11-1 record; directs last-minute drive to defeat University of Georgia in the Sugar Bowl; comes in fourth in Heisman Trophy voting

1983   Is sixth quarterback picked in first round of a famous NFL draft; signs multimillion dollar contract with Miami Dolphins; becomes first rookie ever to have highest quarterback rating in AFC and first rookie quarter-back ever to start in the Pro Bowl

1984   Has greatest season ever by a quarterback, setting records for completions, yards, and touchdown passes

1985   Plays in only Super Bowl, losing to Joe Montana's San Francisco 49ers

1993   Suffers Achilles tendon injury that ends his record streak of 145 consecutive game starts

1994   In first game back after the injury, throws for 473 yards and 5 touchdowns in thrilling win over New England Patriots; leads Dolphins to best season in years, nearly bringing them again to the Super Bowl

STATISTICS

DAN MARINO

YEAR	G	ATT	CMP	YDS	PCT	TD	INT	RTG
1983	11	296	173	2210	58.4	20	6	96.0
1984	16	564	362	5084	64.2	48	17	108.9
1985	16	567	336	4137	59.3	30	21	84.1
1986	16	623	378	4746	60.7	44	23	92.5
1987	12	444	263	3245	59.2	26	13	89.2
1988	16	606	354	4434	58.4	28	23	80.8
1989	16	550	308	3997	56.0	24	22	76.9
1990	16	531	306	3563	57.6	21	11	82.6
1991	16	549	318	3970	57.9	25	13	85.8
1992	16	554	330	4116	59.6	24	16	85.1
1993	5	150	91	1218	60.7	8	3	95.9
1994	16	615	385	4453	62.6	30	17	89.2
TOTALS	172	6049	3604	45173	59.6	328	185	88.3

G	Games
ATT	Attempts
CMP	Completions
YDS	Yards
PCT	Percentage
TD	Touchdowns
INT	Interceptions
RTG	Quarterback Rating

RECORDS SET:

MOST COMPLETIONS, SEASON: 385

MOST YARDS, SEASON: 5,084

MOST TOUCHDOWN PASSES, SEASON: 48

MOST GAMES OVER 300 YARDS PASSING, SEASON: 9

MOST GAMES OVER 400 YARDS PASSING, SEASON: 4

MOST SEASONS WITH AT LEAST 20 TOUCHDOWN PASSES: 11

MOST SEASONS WITH AT LEAST 3,000 YARDS PASSING: 10

MOST CONSECUTIVE SEASONS WITH AT LEAST 3,000 YARDS PASSING: 9

MOST CONSECUTIVE STARTS AT QUARTERBACK: 145

MOST GAMES WITH FOUR TOUCHDOWN PASSES, CAREER: 18

MOST GAMES WITH FIVE TOUCHDOWN PASSES, CAREER: 6

SUGGESTIONS FOR FURTHER READING

O'Brien, Jim. "*Dan Marino.*" Pittsburgh Press Magazine, December 27, 1981.

Miami Dolphins Media Guides, 1985–1994. University of Pittsburgh Media Guides, 1980–1982.

ABOUT THE AUTHOR

Barry Wilner has been a sports writer for the *Associated Press* for 20 years. In that time, he has covered the Super Bowl, Olympics, World Cup, Stanley Cup finals, and many other major sporting events. He has written books on hockey, soccer, swimming, and Olympic sports. He lives in Garnerville, NY, with his wife, Helene, daughters Nicole, Jamie, and Tricia, and son Evan.

INDEX

PICTURE CREDITS

AP/World Wide Photo: 2, 8, 11, 20, 22, 33, 35, 44, 47; UPI/Bettman: 25, 28, 30, 36, 41, 42, 50, 56, 59; Courtesy Dan Marino: 14, 16.